I0810775

# essays
# on kitchens

# essays on kitchens

Klara Czerniewska-Andryszczyk
Olga Drenda
Sarah Dorkenwald
Claudia Banz
Jörg Wiesel
Agata Szydłowska
Anna Carnick

edited by:
Ania Rosinke
Maciej Chmara

Spector Books
Leipzig 2019

# Between Aesthetics and Performativity: Contexts of a Culinary Experience

Klara Czerniewska-Andryszczyk

Ania Rosinke's and Maciej Chmara's creative practice – what the duo call conceptual design – seems to invite parallels with phenomena in the field of contemporary art. Focusing on experiences rather than things or services that are to be used, it can be analyzed in categories drawn from the field of aesthetics or art theory, relating to the multifaceted category of "form" rather than by purely pragmatic and technical criteria of functionality, aptitude, economy or ergonomics – especially since these seem perfectly elaborated and achieved anyway. If the context of relational aesthetics is applicable to the duo's approach, it is because their projects strongly resemble the oeuvre of the Thai artist Rirkrit Tiravanija, most famous for creating installations and shows involving cooking in the gallery context – thus highlighting the situation of people brought together by a shared interest. It is not what you see that is important but what takes place between people, as the artist has famously stated. Tiravanija's work has been cited as the epitome of what French art critic Nicolas Bourriaud defined in his seminal essay *Relational Aesthetics* in 1998: "Rirkrit Tiravanija organises a dinner in a collector's home, and leaves him all the ingredients required to make a Thai soup. Philippe Parreno invites a few people to pursue their favourite hobbies on May Day, on a factory assembly line. Vanessa Beecroft dresses some twenty women in the same way, complete with a red wig, and the visitor merely gets a glimpse of them through the doorway. Maurizio Cattelan feeds rats on "bel paese" cheese and sells them as multiples, or exhibits recently robbed safes. In a Copenhagen square, Jes Brinch and Henrik Plenge Jacobsen install an upturned bus that causes a rival riot in the city [...] One could add many other names and works to such a list. Anyhow, the liveliest factor that is played out on the chessboard of art has to do with interactive, user-friendly and relational concept." "When Jens Hanning broadcasts funny stories in Turkish through a loudspeaker in a Copenhagen square (Turkish Jokes, 1994), he produces in that split second a micro-community, one made up of immigrants brought together by collective laughter which upsets their exile situation, formed in relation to the work and in it", he continues. What Maciej Chmara and Ania Rosinke proposed with their *Mobile Hospitality* was just that: "an arena of exchange", creating a "meaningful moment" – to use some more catchphrases from Bourriaud. Now that collecting experiences, and instantly flushing them into our self-generated stream of online data seems natural in our post-virtual lives, the concept of gathering strangers around a shared table still sounds quite vanguard. Would you perhaps like to sit next to your Uber Eats delivery guy?

Offering food and drink is a gift, an act that evokes a sense of gratefulness. Sometimes, however, it can be seen as a gesture of charity, and thus, to use Pierre Bourdieu's nomenclature, mark a hierarchical symbolically violent relationship between the giver and the receiver. Offering food among equals is a different story. It induces relaxation and invites a good vibe among the group of participants. "Hospitality" seems to be the right word here: the emphasis moves from the object (a physical kitchen) to the feeling of cosiness it evokes. Ania Rosinke and Maciej Chmara conceived *Mobile Hospitality* in 2011. It was first presented at Potenziale Feldkirch in an Austrian town bordering Switzerland and Liechtenstein. In response to the situation, the duo decided to prepare food and drink for the visitors to stimulate their interaction. For chmara.rosinke, the project was a stepping stone: not only did they travel the world and cook in their mobile kitchen on various occasions and for different audiences, but they also showcased the project in exhibitions and managed to place it in notable museum collections (thus changing its status from a tool or service to a museified object); they received important design prizes, and, last but not least, launched new projects, all revolving around the issues of food, eating, and mobility – or "nomadism", as we, the design-crowd, liked to call it back then.

In 1921, five years before coming up with what we now know as the *Frankfurter Küche*, Margarete Schütte-Lihotzky called for a modernization and rationalization of kitchens. In her article published in *Schlesisches Heim* magazine, she cited the model of railway restaurant cars, which, according to Finn Arne Jorgensen, was a "compact concept that had been well tested in practice". Technically speaking, chmara.rosinke's *Mobile Hospitality* is a minimalist, mobile, self-made outdoor kitchen unit. As its famous ancestor, it was built on the premise of indispensable downscaling, in order for all the components – the kitchen with stove and sink, the foldable table and stools – to fit onto one EUR-pallet for convenient transportation. This approach welcomes associations with ingenious, iconic and standardized design solutions for eating on the go, such as special food trolleys in trains or planes; kitchen interiors in either tiny working-class apartments or aboard luxury yachts; the ubiquitous carts, wagons and trucks offering more or less fancy street food, such as hot dogs (or, in Germany, Currywurst), ice cream, etc..

In contrast to such street food connotations, though, the *Mobile Hospitality* kitchen is anything but so-called "standard". As Ania Micińska notes "The DIY elements inspire awe thanks to their playfulness and simplicity – for instance the water system for washing fruit and vegetables is made out of watering cans, a hose, and a foot-powered pump." Clearly a statement of the duo's fascination with DIY and vernacular design, which they have proven on several occasions, including an exhibition "NOMADIC FURNITURE 3.0 – New Liberated Living" at the MAK in Vienna (2013).

How on the other hand does *Mobile Hospitality* resonate with the term "food design"? When we think of food design, we tend to think of the work of Martí Guixé, Marije Vogelzang or Martin Hablesreiter and Sonja Stummerer from Honey and Bunny, who question our notions about how food is supposed to look, taste, smell, sound, how it is served, stored, transported, etc. It seems that with *Mobile Hospitality*, chmara.rosinke were not so much thinking about inventing new dishes or forms of food preparation but preoccupied with creating a service or experience rather than a product – an "edible object". Their work thus seems closer to the definition of Eating Design or Food Service Design proposed by Francesca Zampollo, one of the key academic figures in the discipline. According to Zampollo's sub-categorization, Eating Design is multidisciplinary and includes other elements of Food Design such as Design For and With Food, and Food Space Design. "Eating Design is about designing one-off eating situations, which means that it is different from designing permanent services like restaurants and cafés, and it is really about designing those dinners or lunches that happen only once," she states. "The most interesting part of Eating Design is that eating designers have to – but really get to – design everything [...] This means that when it comes to designing for the eating experience, eating designers have absolute control over the vast majority of the aspects that influence it." This rings absolutely true for chmara.rosinke, who, at least at the very beginning of the project, carefully planned every element of their project, from location scouting to building and setting up the kitchen and the stools and table to inventing the menu and cooking the actual meal. Later on, however, once the project gained visibility and recognisability, the pair occasionally collaborated with chefs, too.

As mentioned before, *Mobile Hospitality* triggered other projects focused on cooking. It seems that the one most closely connected to the classic concept of Food Design is *Cucina Futurista 2.0*, the designers' interpretation of Filippo Tommaso Marinetti's

*La Cucina Futurista*, an eating experience in a gallery setting. Here, however, Chmara and Rosinke also did not design the actual food/edible objects, focusing on the realisation of the Design For Food sub-sector: from tables and chairs to utensils and vessels, the unconventional, abstract, geometrical shapes of which determined the shapes and textures of the food prepared by chefs invited to the project. Rejecting the conventionality of a traditional white plate, the designers invented various spheres, cones, and tubes for the chefs to frame their culinary experiments, thus switching their role from designers to actual clients, expecting chefs to come up with solutions in response to the strictly predefined setting.

The mention of *Cucina Futurista 2.0*, which was first presented at the MAK in Vienna in September 2015, brings us to the issue of the "museification" of these design works. As mentioned, editions of *Mobile Hospitality* were presented in various exhibitions and are now part of the permanent collection at the MAK Vienna and the KGM Berlin. This museification usually means that the object is immobilized and cannot be used, and thus its performativity is only signalled, replaced by photographic or video documentation – sometimes through mockups, sketches, and other elements, replacing the experience and the actual use of the project with a historical contextualization. The user thus becomes a viewer, and the act of personally experiencing the project is replaced by a historicization, a testimony of a third party. Museification is one of the strategies of making a project iconic – establishing distance and shifting the narrative from inclusivity to exclusivity. The afterlife of *Mobile Hospitality* is, however, more complex than that – based on the design, chmara.rosinke were commissioned to devise mobile "pop-up" stands or complete pop-up structures for commercial purposes, too. The life of the structure itself continues, despite the various shifts in its function.

Mobile Hospitality 2011

# “Zrób To Sam”: the Legacy of the DIY Approach in Polish Vernacular Creativity

Olga Drenda

DIY furniture is built from available materials, usually raw and inexpensive. Perhaps the most astonishing career of a piece of furniture with a DIY potential is the one of the *Adirondack Chair*, an iconic American outdoor seat with a fan-shaped backrest; plans in various versions are widely available online. The 1903 design was the idea of Thomas Lee, who made simple garden chairs for his relatives and shared the idea with Harry Bunnell, a carpenter who eventually patented the brilliantly simple invention as *Westport Chair* (allegedly without sharing the information with the original inventor). Eventually, the accessibility of the construction led to a diffusion of the idea. The *Adirondack Chair* was designed for outdoors; in Polish vernacular creativity, too, the "sanctuary of nature", a garden allotment, is the realm of DIY. Anthropologist Roch Sulima called these cooperative micro-gardens, often located in close proximity to city centres, a space "between paradise and trash". Found materials, objects made of fragments of broken furniture, repurposed industrial leftovers (here, fruit boxes and pallets as elements for furniture units clearly had a long career before the 2010s DIY hype, in a true Autoprogettazione manner) are typical of these areas, where the sheds themselves are often built out of "rehabilitated" pieces of junk. The second life given to materials and objects is especially visible there, although recently this is slowly giving way to prefabricated garden sheds and furniture bought in supermarkets, along with a taste for "meta-nature", controlled greenery symbolised by neatly cut grass and a row of thujas.

In order to understand the specific nature of the Polish school of vernacular creativity, we need to examine its social and historical background. In Western Europe and the US, regions where the Industrial Revolution has left its mark earlier, the movement towards conscious development of one's own creativity and building one's own belongings out of raw or reused material reaches back into the early 20th century with its particular mix of technological development and back-to-nature sentiments, whereas Poland had remained a rural or semi-rural country until the mid-20th century, with the most radical shift taking place in the post-WW II People's Republic of Poland when the newly established communist state invested in rapid industrialisation, prompting the exodus of millions of people from the countryside into expanding cities and new estates (such as Nowa Huta) in pursuit of employment in heavy industries. Despite this, a large part of the country kept living in conditions that resembled the early 20th century world projected into the 1970s, as demonstrated by Zofia Rydet's photographs from her famous series *Sociological Record*. More importantly, people, also those who had moved to the city, had stuck with rural habits and ways of life for some time, even in tenement estates designed in a functionalist spirit – or somewhat functionalist in their intention at least, with mixed results.

Until the mid-20th century, the form-follows-function principle had been adopted in Polish rural cottages for obvious reasons – scarcity of resources and available technologies. Anthropologist Claude Lévi-Strauss called the propensity to make practical and creative use of objects at hand, within close range (and thus the habit of putting them to often unusual, unexpected use) *bricolage*, a term perhaps closest to *tinkering*. This spirit is as typical of the DIY movement as it is of the way developing societies function. The necessity of rational and efficient management of resources, of space arrangement, of one's time and effort made this approach common. Bread ovens were built in a way that not only permitted the preparation of food, but also provided heating for the room and a pleasant and comfortable, warm sleeping space (on a small bed-bench next to the oven or on top of it (idyllic depictions of country homes usually include a cat cosily sleeping there). The construction was multifunctional and versatile in a way reminiscent of DIY kitchen designs – not in terms of movability or construction (as it often needed support from a qualified stove-maker), but in terms of the use of space and lateral thinking. The same manner of thinking was seemingly applied to the space of functionalist flats into which the rural families were moving in the 1950s: completely rejecting the prearranged layout of the flat, they often repurposed the rooms in a makeshift manner, adapting them to their own habits and customs. In a country house, the space was often divided into a working space – the kitchen, which also served as a living room, bedroom, small workshop and a more relaxed room for the children) and a festive space – a clean, decorated parlour furnished with more expensive things and used for special occasions, such as formal hospitality or celebrations. Hence, many people were trying to fit their entire lives into the small space of the kitchen in their apartments, completely ignoring the pre-fitted living room. Sometimes there were even attempts to turn the flats into micro-farms, with chickens kept in bathrooms or on the balconies. Such customization against the grain of predesigned spaces reveals how commonplace the idea of repurposing something according to one's own preference was – and also how common the necessary skills were.

In Polish, the phrase DIY – Do It Yourself – is translated directly as "zrób to sam". Incidentally, this was also the title of one of the most popular TV programmes in the 1980s, a time of deep economic crisis and shortages in Poland. Not only was the phrase commonly used – probably as early as in English – but, more importantly, the concept itself, and the spirit behind it, was put into practice by thousands of people who were sometimes unaware that they were, in fact, part of the DIY movement. The TV programme, hosted by Adam Słodowy, a *bricoleur extraordinaire* and talented ex-military and constructor, presented various constructions in a way that made making them seem very simple. Słodowy also published a number of books dedicated to popularizing the idea of DIY. But he wasn't the only one: magazines such as *Mój Dom*, *Zrób To Sam* or *Horyzonty Techniki* showcased DIY ideas, not only those of the engineers in the editorial staff, but also of readers who wanted to exchange advice or share their successes. In addition to simple designs in the Autoprogettazione spirit, these titles also promoted advanced engineering – building one's own kitchen appliances, heating systems, plumbing, radios etc. The popularity of technical education and arts and crafts classes in schools facilitated the DIY movement – driven by necessity and economic conditions but also by personal ambition. One notable example involved a reader who built his own little house, carrying all the necessary materials from one town to another on a suburban bus.

This particular type of creativity thrived especially in the 1980s. The lack of basic materials caused by an economic crisis within planned economy conditions in 1980s Poland encouraged many people to take things into their own hands. Revisiting period newscasts reveals missing links in the chain of production and distribution on the most banal levels – even tiny but necessary elements like screws or nails were often scarce which would often bring production to a halt or mean that products would be made and sold that would simply not function at all. In these conditions, furniture and home appliances became highly sought-after goods. The idea of homemade creativity and handicrafts was welcomed with support from the state-owned press and publishers as it helped to "keep calm and carry on" in an unfavourable situation, and – presumably – helped to alleviate some of the frustration caused by the constant chase for basic home appliances. Magazines dedicated to home design shifted from the futuristic optimism and clean functionalism of the 1960s and 1970s towards sobriety, thrift and the reuse of recycled or leftover goods. In these conditions, the motivational slogan from the era of prosperity, the 1970s – "A Pole can do it!" – acquired an ironic spin as they now had no other choice.

Currently, the popularity of IKEA and its Polish twins Agata Meble and Black Red White suggests that the Poles may be tired of DIY and relax into a bliss of satisfied consumption of prefabricated projects which don't leave a wide margin for individual invention. Yet, at the same time, the popularity of crafts workshops, a certain resurgence in technical education, a growing trend of returning towards thrift and an efficient use of resources – this time not out of poverty but out of responsibility for the environment – seems to demonstrate that the spirit of vernacular creativity in Poland is very much alive, albeit under different circumstances and out of different motivations. Numbers seem to support such conclusions: according to a 2016 survey, a significant number of Poles – as many as 73% – make small repairs and build things themselves not only for practical reasons but also for pleasure.

## DIY Vertical Kitchen 2013

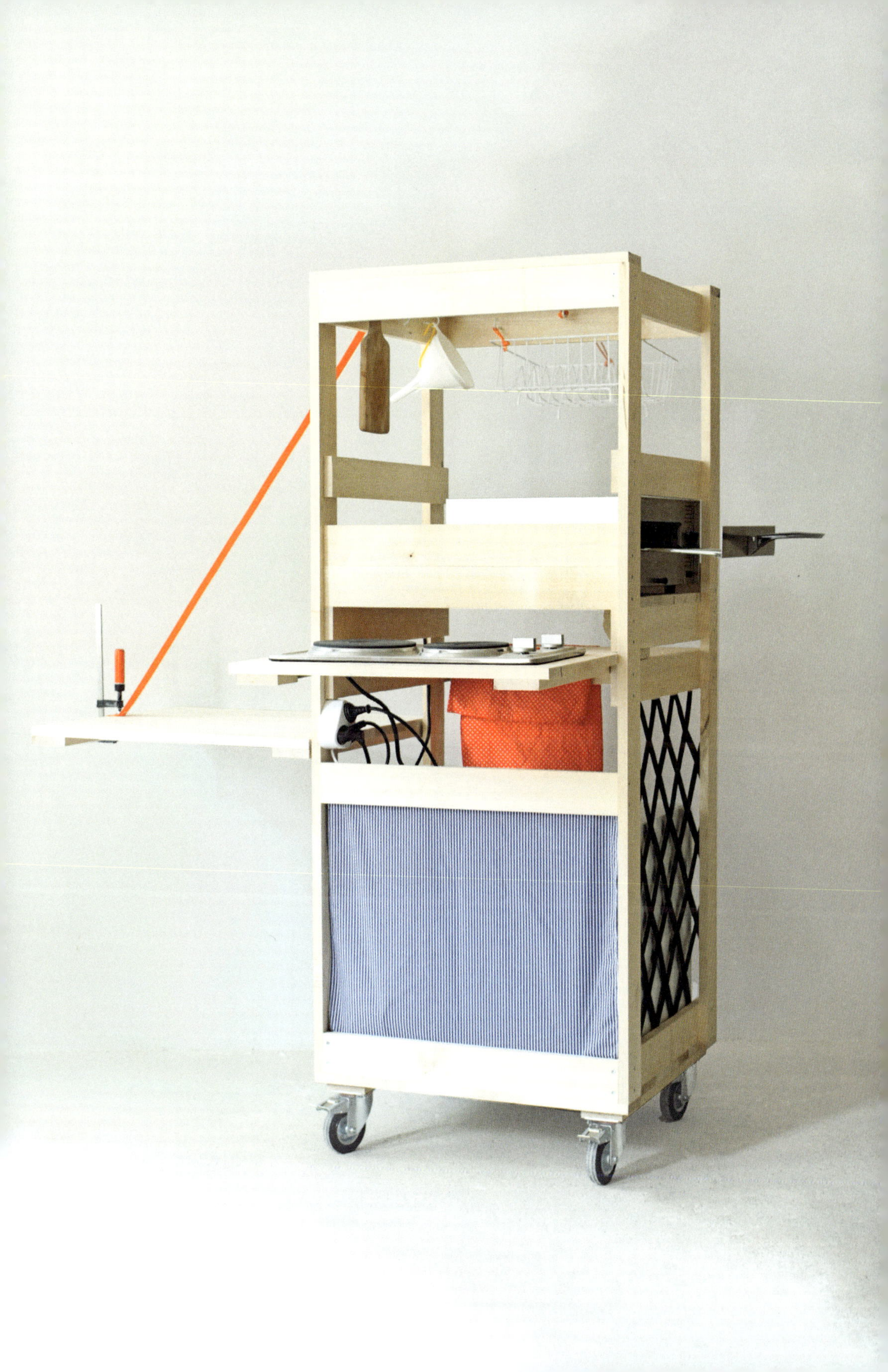

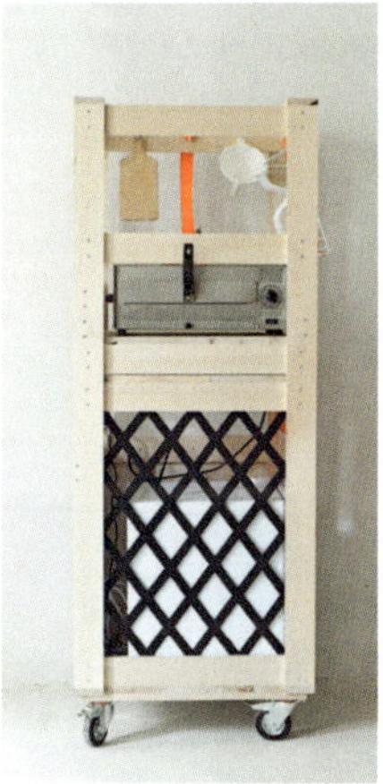

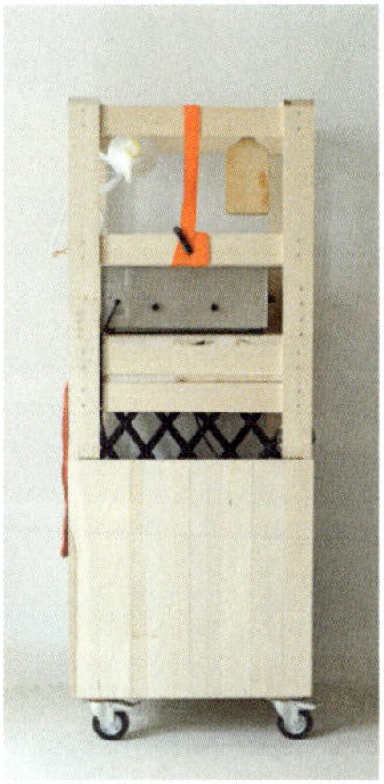

# The Kitchen as a Mirror of Our Society

Sarah Dorkenwald

Kitchens have always been the expression of a concept of society. A trip through the decades shows the use of kitchens in social context and illustrates how kitchen design and lifestyles have always influenced each other. Technological developments define the design, but in addition, the rediscovery of cooking as a social activity, a new relationship to nature, and the wish to eat healthy and sustainable food are characteristics of our current understanding of the kitchen as a living space. Designers and the industry are envisioning the kitchen of the future on the basis of present-day phenomena.

*Kitchens Along TeLa* is the name of the art project of photographer Verena Hägler, whose photo series of private kitchen spaces along the Tegernseer Landstraße – an important artery of a Munich neighbourhood undergoing gentrification – offers objective and documentary insights, but also a curious and voyeuristic glimpse of domestic lives and individual living arrangements. These kitchens with their diverse and varied furnishings serve as cooking spaces and production sites, extended dining and living rooms, storage spaces or even as music rooms, and are one thing above all: a social meeting place as well as the identity generating heart of the home. The individual design of these kitchen spaces full of personal objects works like a seismograph and allows us to deduct a multi-layered image of society. Diverse lifestyles and ways of living are indicative of social, economic, technological, and aesthetic conditions.

Judging from the paintings of old masters, it seems there has always been something of a cosiness and romanticism about the kitchen. Whether a farmers' kitchen or a feudal one, the open fireplace or the ceiling-high tiled stove with a little bench, both were the warm heart of a spacious and central room where servants and family members met to cook, eat, chat, pickle vegetables, sleep, bathe, or wash their clothes. Domestic life revolved around the kitchen cum living space. With industrialization and the associated formation of a bourgeois middle class, this live-in kitchen was replaced by the dining room with a breakfast kitchen and a corner sofa. In the bourgeois parlour, cooking and eating were largely separated activities. Those who were able to afford it had live-in servants who took care of kitchen chores in the background. At the same time, the proletariat, the labourers who migrated to the cities to work in the new factories, lived in cramped and poor conditions. Kitchens in the newly built tenements were rudimentary spaces, often without a window, badly ventilated and ill-lit, and with deplorable hygiene. In Berlin, three quarters of a million people lived in these mass-constructed courtyard apartments and tenement blocks around 1910.

In the 1920s, the first modern social housing estates were developed. The trend towards the nuclear family, the requirement of spatial efficiency, and a new understanding of the role of women were reflected in architecture and floor plans. The idea was to rationalize housekeeping and relieve the burden on women with a functionally furnished kitchen, in most cases a small, separate room. One remarkable example is the central or community kitchen Adolf Loos planned for the Friedensstadt estate in Vienna in 1921. Instead of providing an individual kitchen for each household, he designed a large communally used kitchen for several units. Thus it was easier for the women to participate in community life. It was women's rights activist Lily Braun who had the idea to create a centrally operated kitchen in order to liberate women from their daily domestic chores, an alternative concept to the emerging mass housing with its tiny units. Loos's concept seems to have been too progressive for its time and had little impact. Instead, what proved to be the most influential kitchen design, and the prototype of the modern kitchen, was the – widely known – *Frankfurter Küche* by Austrian architect Margarete Schütte-Lihotzky, which was developed in 1927 for the housing estates of New Frankfurt.

While the central kitchen of Loos's single kitchen house could serve as a place of social exchange, shared experiences, pleasure and cooking experiments, an approach that is revived today in cooperative residential construction and movements of communal creation or commoning, the housewife in Lihotzky's small kitchen mainly worked in a result-oriented and purposeful manner. cooked. It took some time until this idea of the kitchen as a closed single-purpose space with standardized built-in elements was challenged again. In the kitchen units designed for the Unité d'Habitation in Marseille by Charlotte Perriand and Le Corbusier in 1949, the narrow space was at least opened up towards the dining space by a counter, which meant women were less isolated in the activities attributed to them.

The phase of a single-purpose kitchen only began to give way to much more visionary living concepts in the 1960s. Designers addressed phenomena like limited housing in cities, single lifestyles or an increasingly mobile society, and planned kitchens that weren't necessarily bound to a specific space. The Cucina Minima by Italian designer Joe Colombo, designed in 1964 for the kitchen manufacturer Boffi and still in their programme, reduced the kitchen to a kind of cube on wheels. This mini kitchen unit with pull-out elements, integrated mini fridge, storage systems and cooking plate can find its space anywhere there is a power supply. Where this kitchen still aimed for functionality, Luigi Colani's 1970 space age kitchen became only a concept of a kitchen. In this futuristic 'ball kitchen' designed for the innovative kitchen manufacturer Poggenpohl, all appliances and cupboards were arranged horizontally and vertically around the centre with a revolving chair. Individual and material merged into a single affirmative plastic high-tech world. What was served was – at a pinch, packet soups and tinned pasta. But nevertheless, cooking was no longer regarded as a professional matter or the territory of the housewife, but as a communicative hobby and integral extension of the living room – cooking for everyone.

While Stefan Wewerka reduced the kitchen to his *Kitchen Tree*, the most minimal sense of a cooking space, in 1984, Otl Aicher placed the kitchen table in the centre and planned it as a detached kitchen island and workbench. His inspiration came from professional kitchens. The open-plan kitchen with its fluid transition into the living and dining areas now is a meeting point and pivot for joint cooking, good conversations, and sensual and appreciative culinary experiences, and also provides space for professional appliances and equipment. It is not a rational minimal solution that considers cooking to be a necessary daily burden, but a prestigious luxury solution with a plethora of ideas completing the image of the kitchen. Otl Aicher's study *The Kitchen is for Cooking. The End of an Architectural Doctrine* for kitchen manufacturer Bulthaup triggered a paradigm shift beginning in the 1980s. Finally, the act of cooking and eating as a social, sensual and enjoyable experience came to the foreground. In the new kitchen plans, cooking was to become a shared event and the kitchen a space of natural communication. Of course this generous attitude is not within everybody's means, which is maybe a reason for the steady increase in offers of urban cooking studios and cooking workshops to be rented for joint activities with friends. In keeping with our service-oriented society, cookery classes, event cooking, cooking as a team building event, or recipes and ingredients will be provided as well. Welfare organisations like Caritas make use of the therapeutic effect of cooking together.

A longing for sensuality, manual work and DIY, healthy diets and rootedness, and for cooking as a social experience seems to be common; nevertheless, we cook less and less due to lack of time, convenience, lack of knowledge, creativity, or space, and alternative offers like convenience and fast food, delivery services and ready-to-eat products. And although the Thermomix, Vorwerk's miracle cooking machine, with its look of a product of 1960s science fiction has been around for more than twenty years, it might be taken as a symbol of our current dilemma. When all cooking functions like stirring, chopping, weighing, roasting or steaming are united in one machine, we lose our appetite for cooking. So is there no more need for a kitchen? Is the kitchen obsolete after all this experimentation?

The question of the future kitchen remains open. Will the kitchen of the future really be smart and green? An ecological and quite radical design comes from the London studio vhm design, who designed a household as a biologically closed circuit with their Microbial Home for Philips Design in 2011. There is neither lost heat nor waste, everything is recycled. They developed new kitchen appliances like the *Paternoster*, an upcycling machine for plastic waste. Fungal cultures decompose shredded plastic waste, on which edible fungi can grow provided the plastic does not contain poisonous substances. The dining table is inlaid with clay pots for natural food refrigeration, and the gas stove is fuelled with biogas produced by the bacteria decomposing organic waste. A more contradictory future concept is the digital kitchen version by the design company IDEO, which includes an interactive table that suggests recipes based on household leftovers. With the help of sensors that scan available edibles, these inspirations for cooking aim to avoid that food is thrown away.

Whatever idea of the kitchen will evolve in the future, this space will always be the expression of our personal preferences, modes of life and social needs.

Community Cooking Kitchen 2014

Community
Cooking
Caritas
&Du

# Time for Oneself or Designing Nostalgia

Claudia Banz

The separation of work and leisure is one of the main characteristics of conventional Western existences. Polarizing experiences and feelings of fragmentation and alienation already were basic constants of Modernity. What emerged was a concept of the country as a counter-image to the city, as an emotionally charged place of leisure and thus a cure-all for the negative consequences of urban civilization. However, the glorification of nature as a retreat did not originate in the 20th century. As early as the Rococo, the so-called bucolic idyll emerged as a pastoral topos that reflected the nostalgia of the middle class and defined nature as a source of conventional ideas of culture and as a bourgeois space of experience. An important facet of this pastoral topos was the allegedly simple and honest life in nature's abode as opposed to the city.

The rapid development of digitalization and the ensuing radical transformation of our ways of living constitute a new caesura. Big data, the Internet of Things, or robotics, to cite only a few phenomena, cause extensive upheavals in our societies and most importantly transform our concept of time. The enormous potential of digital modernity oscillates between making our everyday lives easier and total dependency on the machinery of the information age. Digitalization not only signifies revolution but also evolution. Even today we are confronted with the negative effects of hyperconnectivity: for many, it has long become an addiction. In this context, "time for oneself" acquires another fundamental purpose. It no longer just means being off work, but going offline. Leisure thus becomes a digital time-out. The future place of leisure is also a place of deconnectivity, for offline is the new online.

Against this backdrop, work and leisure experience another shift of meaning. While the Western concept of time may be condensed into the motto “time is money”, the current counter-concept to the rational work ethos reads “slow work”. We are talking about a conflation of business and leisure, of bleisure. The work-life balance ideals of a new generation of urban digital nomads come with a renaissance of the pastoral. In the context of a post-growth society and an increasing scarcity of resources, our food production systems and methods are put to the test and urgently require a food revolution. In the 1980s, an ecological movement emerged and its activists emphasized regional sourcing, sustainability, deceleration, a simple and primarily self-sufficient life close to nature, and opting out of the capitalist treadmill. The current movement of the next food generation differs from its parent generation mainly in that its position is less an “either/or”, but has assimilated a healthy and natural diet as a key lifestyle issue. This also involves adopting elements of do-it-yourself and self-supply as common practices of urban life.

The crafted versus the industrially made mass product: between these poles, a new but fundamentally old hierarchy of values is negotiated that not only leads to a revitalization of culinary traditions from a variety of cultures and outmoded traditional skills of doing things oneself, but also challenges the ethics of things as a whole. Since the Arts and Crafts movement, crafts per se are associated with the idea of the morally good and honest, with the practice of ‘true experience’. Crafts are defined by the past because every artisanal discipline has a history that is inscribed into its particular objects. In this respect, practicing a craft is a statement because it is an attempt to unite hand and head, physical work and thought, on an equal standing once more.

With *Time for Oneself*, craftsmanship is celebrated in its purest form. A total of seven artisans have worked on the set, from a brushmaker to a restorer of swords. It also features a sophisticated functionality: The backpack can be transformed into a stool and is closed with the cutting board. In the bucket, one can light a fire; it serves as an oven or as a smoking chamber and is equipped with an adjustable air inlet. It also doubles as the container for transporting the other components of the set: a pan and a bowl, a leather and a linen cloth, handheld angling gear, salt and pepper casters, a fish knife and a hunting knife, a brush, a spatula and a leather strap to fasten everything and carry it as a backpack. The materials used are ashwood, stainless steel and burnished black steel, and pig's bristles for the brush.

chmara.rosinke are part of the generation of designer-makers who utilize the cultural force inherent in crafts for an innovative design – innovative less in the sense of technological progress, but as an identity-generating moment. Even though individual items from the set of *Time for Oneself*, for instance the fish knife, are designed from models from their personal childhood memories, they also touch the collective memory due to their contemporary archetypal feel. Angling, too, is one of the fond personal experiences from childhood days. It stands at the heart of *Time for Oneself*: as a meditative examination of instinct and primal drives, as a leisure activity associated with deceleration and closeness to nature, and not least as an ecologically sustainable version of self-supply with fresh fish. The mini kitchen in the form of the bucket described above allows immediate preparation. Here, too, the primal drives of hunting and gathering evoke archaic images. For French sociologist Claude Lévi-Strauss, the cooking of food marks the first cultural act of the human being, and thus the origin of civilization and crafts. The bucket for lighting a fire implies the campfire, which can also produce community, for cooking is also one of the most ancient models of open source work.

The angler is the new protagonist of the bucolic Rococo idyll that exposed the bourgeois nostalgia for a balanced life in harmony with nature. However, the age of digital modernity has seen a fundamental change, not only in the social but mostly the economic framework. Speaking of the responsibility of designers against this background, the strategy of nostalgia as applied by chmara.rosinke, not only in *Time for Oneself*, appears as one possible path for a future-oriented design practice: this is no superficial, anonymous retro design or the ossification of a supposed tradition, but a conscious aesthetic attitude that promotes urgently needed sustainable and resource-friendly production methods for our everyday objects; that is able to evoke emotional values through the intrinsic value of the material and thus contributes to the durability of the objects in both senses, and in addition establishes a new, positive atmospheric relation between the human being and their environment. *Time for Oneself* is a multi-faceted definition of the luxury of time as a balanced relation of human being AND nature, between contemplation AND consumption – in short, as a return to essentials.

Time for Oneself 2014

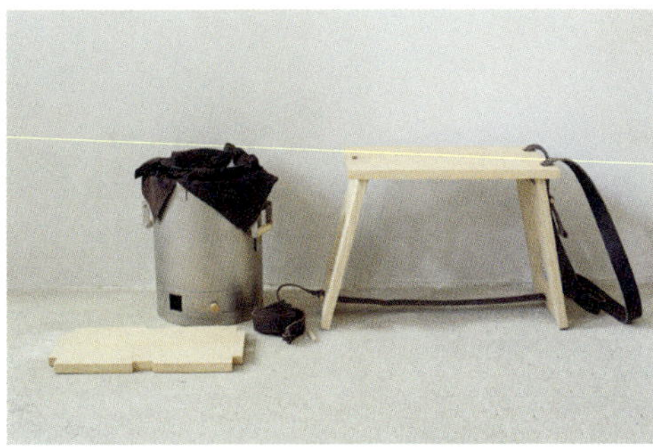

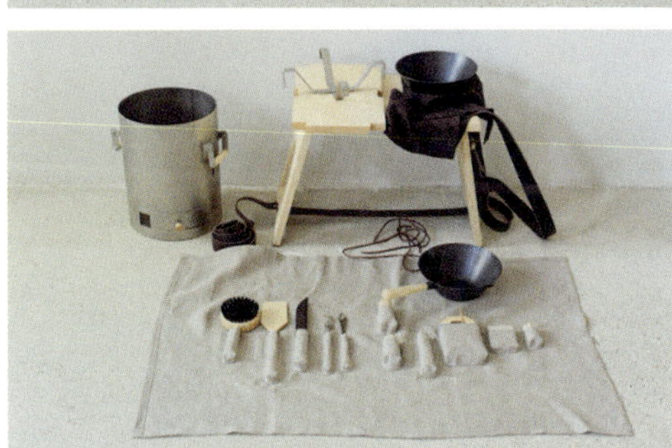

# Mobile Immobility. The Fourth Wall of the Kitchen

Jörg Wiesel

A visit to Thomas Imbusch's new restaurant *100/200* in Hamburg in March 2019: in the centre, a Molteni stove, a unique specimen, specially built for Imbusch. The social aspects of the meal include cooks, guests, sommeliers and service; it is after all a matter of restoring oneself. Like the food on display, you are restored, because that's what the word "restaurant" stands for. Imbusch and his team uncover the semantic core of the restaurant, which in their eyes is real. We are sitting in a room in which everything happens, a stove around which everything revolves, water at 100°C that alters food and a 200°C hot oven that cooks everything. But this kitchen is immobile.

This is even more than what has recently been called Nova Regio Cuisine. What was literally obvious in the region became a precious resource in the culinary eyes of the chefs who integrated the products into the calculation of their alimentary and gastronomic practice. The techniques of Nova Regio Cuisine often derive their effect from non-European, mostly Asian cultures and the strategies of molecular cuisine, in addition to the advanced reflection of biochemical processes such as roasting, cooking, caramelising, smoking, fermenting, distilling or charring. Nicolaj van der Meulen and I have described the significant change in this type of cuisine and gastronomy as a culinary turn. Within this turn, cooking can no longer be characterized as artistic (artist cooking), but as an aesthetic practice exercised by society, not least in order to participate in the possibilities of artistic creativity and its mechanisms of subjectification. The Icelandic artist Olafur Eliasson, who works in Berlin, has published a cookbook that shows his team in contact with cooks such as Alice Waters and René Redzepi. As a culinary turn, we thus defined a cultural transformation that, as a complex structure and as a dispositive, reassembles and condenses the fields of culinary arts, gastronomy, agriculture, aesthetics, food, and nutrition in a specific way. It is not so much a methodological-scientific turn, but a significant change in social engagement with those fields that can be diagnosed, and an attention to culinary topics. It should be emphasized that especially what takes place in the new formation of different levels that coordinate the topic of cooking/eating is a strong visual, aesthetic and rhetorical accentuation of the rural space from which the regional products originate. Whether as "culinary materialism" (Jakob Tanner) which links the food modified by genetic engineering to the optimization of human labour, or as culinary materialism which defines cooking in the course of the renaissance of "speculative realism" or the speculative turn to the material-saturated exploration of an origin of the world: our formula of the culinary turn as an aesthetic practice of cooking reflects and challenges socio-political as well as philosophical transformations. The further development of Nouvelle Cuisine and Molecular Cuisine at the end of the 20th and the beginning of the 21st century established the position of a cuisine oriented towards regionality, seasonality and culinary heritage (cultural heritage, cultural property). The menus of avant-garde natural cuisine, which are based on sophisticated concepts and high-quality ingredients, can – we suspected – be understood as visual and culinary representations of rural areas, which vary the taste of the elements to the extent that they specifically weigh the biochemical processes involved in cooking. Cooks such as Andoni Luis Aduriz, René Redzepi, Magnus Nilsson and Stefan Wiesner have researched and analysed the vitality and attraction of rural areas.

Not so Thomas Imbusch: he breaks this paradigm and is restorative. In Imbusch, something is restored, but it is not initially the lost taste of a fish, a fruit or the oyster's rag or beard. It is the highly staged process in the use of cooking techniques, the artisanal practice of which is exemplified in the immobile stove and the pots by Le Creuset and clearly demonstrates that the oyster beard is edible (and even tasty). And this restoration in the restaurant is staged theatrically. The immobility of the Molteni stove provokes the motoric and physical mobility of the guests, whose feelings are valued to an extraordinary extent. Thomas Imbusch and his team are staging a theatre of emotions that aims to allow the affectivity (ecstasy) of cooking to be perceived by the guests. The ecstasy of cooking induces an ecstasy of enjoyment and recreates an experience of culinary delights believed lost. Two numbers suffice for him to create a solid basis for food, emotions and ecstasy: 100 and 200 – these temperatures bring water to boiling point and the stove to full blast. The restorative moment consists of allowing the moment when food was not questioned but simply enjoyed to be reexperienced within a framework of culinary and gastronomic sustainability. In this respect, it is also a restorative reenactment – at least this is the idea. Because everything is eaten – in the kitchen and at the table: "foot broth", "innards' ragout", "liver sauce" or "skin snack". The guest's curiosity about what they is eating is directed towards the immobile stove in the centre of the restaurant by sophisticated lighting technology. Staged like a fetish, its immobility seems almost sacral; you have to walk around it, it structures the movements of the cooks (on the gallery) as well as the motoric skills of the guests, who re-experience the products of its temperatures (100/200). It is almost as in Denis Diderot's "Parodoxe sur le Comédien": the cooks play behind a fourth wall that separates the stage from the audience (gallery); the claimed naturalness (authenticity) of the restorative activities can only be had at the price of their rhetorical and theatrical production. Already Diderot had a complex structure of observation in mind: it is the Fourth Wall that "turns the viewer into someone absent in imagination and therefore into an unobserved observer" (Johannes Lehmann) of the cooks, who pretend not to be observed. But of course they also observe the guests; and very closel at that. But whenever a gaze from the kitchen (over the stove) seeks the audience, it is quickly withdrawn – almost as if it had been caught breaking out of the unity of representation that presents authenticity here. But exactly this moment increases the tension, mobilizes affects. In Diderot's words: the exclusion of emotion (with the actress as with the cook) places the emotions in the things: the stove, the pots, the meat, the beard of the oyster. From there, they become mobile and reach the ecstasy of the guest's food. The setting of the kitchen as "immutable mobile" (Bruno Latour) at Imbusch is caught in the paradoxes of a sophisticated observation device. But this is where we emerge: in digression through (mobile) digestion.

Cucina Futurista 2.0 2015

# The Emancipation of the Kitchen

Agata Szydłowska

In May 1965, the Polish lifestyle magazine *Ty i Ja* praised fitted kitchens: "One of the tendencies of modern domestic architecture has been an integration of an entire apartment with what we used to call the kitchen. The kitchen has gradually been transformed into a laboratory; it has stored more and more appliances with styles to suit every taste. Why shouldn't we therefore think – remaining obstacles, including ventilation aside – about including the kitchen into the normal living area? To transform it into a niche, an annex linked to the living area instead of treating it as the sphere of an enslaved housewife. Additional contributions to the emancipation of this hitherto isolated space are the fact that even men now work in the kitchen, and the lack of servants." Three years earlier, the magazine had argued that "a kitchen is not a shameful space". Within the contemporary social structure, it clarified, in which a servant has become a relic, the kitchen had become a family's domain and a housewife's workplace.

The emancipation of the kitchen as understood in this quotation was threefold. First it meant social emancipation and, quite literally, the disappearance of servants. Obviously, in the People's Republic, where *Ty i Ja* was published, there was no room for the bourgeois and aristocratic habit of having domestic staff; but the tendency was widespread across Europe and anything but new. In his book *Home: A Short History of an Idea*, Witold Rybczyński explains why the kitchen acquired its central place in 17th century Dutch homes with the decreasing number of servants and the transformation of homes into the workplace of housewives. While back in those days in other European countries, kitchens were virtually separate from the rest of the dwelling and rather neglected, in the Netherlands, they played a leading role and housewives took special care of them. This is quite understandable. As long as the kitchen is a place exclusively devoted to servants who have no say, nobody takes an interest in improving it. But as soon as a housewife occupies it, she takes good care of the space, makes generous investments and integrates it into the rest of the home.

In Europe between the two World Wars, the introduction of modern, compact kitchens with a clear connection to the living space also had much to do with progressive social ideas and the disappearance of servants. Barbara Brukalska was an architect who designed kitchen-laboratories for a social housing project, the Warsaw Housing Cooperative. On closer inspection, her drawings show a fashionable lady with a pixie cut working in the kitchen. She definitely is not a servant but a modern working woman who has a job outside the home, maybe the architect herself. Indeed, the architects of the Warsaw Housing Cooperative didn't provide for any special rooms for servants in the progressive, modern but modest apartments they designed. Nonetheless, their middle class occupants were not very keen to abandon their habits and kept domestic service anyway. Since there were no rooms assigned to the servants, they were forced to live in basements, attics, garbage dumpsters or even sleep in bathtubs. Still, the gradual disappearance of servants was a fact, and it had a huge influence on the designs of modern kitchens. Design historian Adrian Forty commented on the idea that domestic appliances were invented as a response to the decline of the servant class. He noted that this idea has been repeated so many times that it's finally become a widely accepted fact, which came in handy both to housewives and to manufacturers of domestic gadgets and equipment.

The emancipation of the kitchen also meant an emancipation of women themselves. Initially, however, the ideas for comfortable, labour-saving kitchens didn't question traditional gender roles. Christine Frederick, an American, was a pioneer of scientific management in the kitchen. Inspired by Frederick Taylor's ideas, to which she was introduced by her husband, she elaborated a precise methodology of time- and energy-saving kitchen design. Her design process was based on research. In her studio-kitchen she conducted experiments with step-saving food preparation processes and investigated hundreds of kitchen products. Her meticulous calculations of the time needed to perform different tasks resulted in a significant rationalization of a woman's work in the kitchen. The time saved on daily chores could be used for the benefit of the family. Frederick's book *The New Housekeeping* (1912) was extraordinarily influential. It was translated into six languages and widely cited by members of the European avant-garde. However, the aesthetics of Frederic's kitchen was still quite conservative, and so was her motivation.

Eventually, a modern, hygienic fitted kitchen-laboratory was developed in Europe within the context of functionalism and the concern for social welfare. Barbara Brukaska's kitchen in the Warsaw Housing Cooperative is a good example, as it was designed as part of the utopian programme of working-class housing and eventually became available for wealthier inhabitants. In Germany, new kitchens were developed as a means to free women from the drudgery of the kitchen and allow them to work outside the home. The most successful realisation of the kitchen-laboratory was the *Frankfurter Küche* designed by Margarete Schütte-Lihotzky, a devoted reader of Christine Frederick's work and an enthusiast of household engineering. This kitchen was developed for a social housing project designed by Ernst May in Frankfurt and eventually was installed in ten thousand apartments. The architect's motivation was clearly progressive. She claimed that "the struggle of women for economic independence and personal development meant that the rationalization of housework was an absolute necessity." Schütte-Lihotzky managed to combine household engineering principles with a highly modern aesthetics and laid the foundations for all later fitted, compact kitchens. The scientific look of these kitchens didn't mean that their architects avoided decisions relating to their styling. Adrian Forty remarked that the middle classes of the late 19$^{th}$ and early 20$^{th}$ centuries became increasingly concerned with cleanliness, which explains the extraordinary success of hygienic spaces, white and smooth, seamless, easily cleaned surfaces. Contrary to this tendency, some of the most influential female designers decided to use colour in their kitchens. The *Frankfurter Küche* had a number of variations and some of them included furnishings in plain, cold colors like blue and green hues. Much more colorful was a compact kitchen designed by Charlotte Perriand and Le Corbusier for his Unité d'Habitation in Marseille. The flat panels used for furnishings came in different colors, forming an abstract geometrical composition.

This exploration of scientific home management was illustrated in *Kitchen Stories*, a film directed by Bent Hamer. The opening scenes show a laboratory where the subjects and their performances are meticulously timed in order to optimise kitchen design. Then a researcher is sent to the field with a mission to put a single male under investigation. This is where the funny part starts: clearly, the kitchen-laboratory was designed for women. Nevertheless, Penny Sparke, a design historian, argues that architects such as Brukalska or Schütte-Lihotzky were in fact agents of "male" aesthetics with its functionalist and modern look and scientific approach.

A more "female" outlook can definitely be found in the post-war American kitchen with a stereotypical domestic goddess in stiletto heels surrounded by streamlined household appliances. This spacious kitchen was also suited to serve as the epicentre of family life, as a journalist observed in *Time Magazine* in 1954: “Since the war, whole houses are virtually being designed around colorful, labor-saving kitchens that can also serve as an all-purpose living space for the family.” This abundance of colours was stimulated by the domestication of new materials, especially plastic. The plethora of different colours and shapes of Tupperware dishes are a good example of this plastic revolution. Modernity and progress not only meant that man could go to the Moon, but also that the American housewife could aspire to the gadgets of her dreams. In 1956, General Motors published a promotional film, *Design for Dreaming*. The main character, an svelte dancer, is taken to a spectacular car show and an even more spectacular ”Kitchen of the Future” which saves the lady’s time not by scientific engineering but by mechanisation by a masked man. The lady is delighted to find she has plenty of time for entertainment. In fact, American post-war kitchens were anything but compact and were demonstrations of abundance and prosperity. They also were the arena of the activities of professional housewives, the place where women could spend their day taking care of their families and homes and chatting with lady neighbours, who also did not work. At least this is the image evoked by pop culture, where frustrated women spend their idle hours in their beautiful kitchens, either chain smoking (*Mad Men*) or planning their escape (*The Hours*).

The first secretary of the Soviet Communist Party, Nikita Khrushchev, had a similar image of women in the American “wonder kitchen”. It became a strange battleground in the Cold War competition. In 1959, after the USSR had launched its first artificial satellite, *Sputnik 1*, the United States organised the American National Exhibition in Moscow. The Americans were fully aware of the fact that they were losing the Cold War competition on the military and space fronts, so they decided to outpace their enemy when it came to the quality of everyday life. The exhibition therefore showed a plethora of American consumer goods with a spectacular wonder kitchen as one of the main attractions. This was the setting of the famous confrontation of the two leaders of the superpowers, Khrushchev and Richard Nixon, known as the Kitchen Debate. Nixon was very proud of this demonstration of wealth and innovation, but Khrushchev was not an easy adversary. He accused American culture of keeping women in the "golden cages" of their huge kitchens while Soviet working women were given compact kitchen-laboratories which saved them time and eventually contributed to their emancipation. "I feel sorry for Americans," said Khrushchev, "judging by your exhibition. Does your life really just consist of kitchens?" The intelligent Soviet leader presented the small, modest kitchens in small and low-quality mass housing as tools for emancipation. He didn't quite go as far as Lenin himself, however, who had proposed in the 1920s to abandon kitchens in general and to replace them with collective dining. In Khrushchev's kitchen, the one who cooked still was a woman, a working woman who, as a result, had two jobs: one outside the home and one in her kitchen.

The real emancipation of the kitchen may ultimately be the emancipation of the very space which became possible thanks to the advent of clean fuels (gas and electricity) in Western Europe and the US after World War I. The author of the article quoted at the beginning proposed to connect the kitchen with the rest of the home. This space would become the heart of family life. After the war, eating in the kitchen became a widely accepted habit. In small apartments, there was no room for a big table and a separate dining room. Small dimensions prevented the inhabitants from sleeping in the kitchen, a common habit before the advent of efficient central heating as the kitchen used to be the warmest in the house. In the following decades, when aesthetics and sophistication of kitchens allowed it, they became directly connected with living rooms. Preparing food and cooking was exposed and cooking became a social activity, even a performative one. What might be the next step of the emancipation of the kitchen? Does an emancipated kitchen necessarily have to be a fitted one? Or could it emancipate itself from the given space and be taken somewhere else, even outside the home?

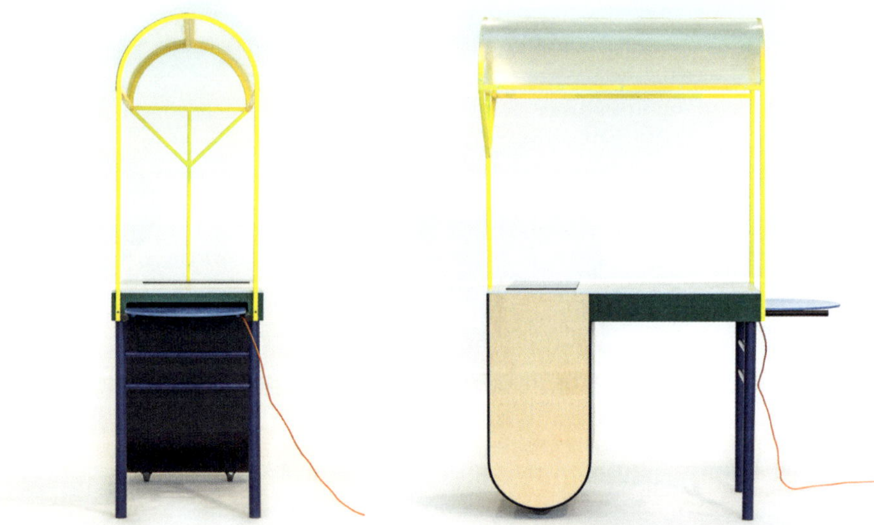

Neo Modernist Kitchen 2018

# Food for Thought: The kitchen series by chmara.rosinke

Anna Carnick

“What if?” is such an inspiring, open-ended question. In the case of the experimental design studio, much of the past decade has been dedicated to exploring the “what ifs” relating to the culture of food and, more specifically, the kitchen. In six major works in a variety of contexts, they have reimagined the structure, functionality, and aesthetics of the kitchen – the physical and symbolic heart of culinary life. And in doing so, they have provided opportunities for the rest of us to reconsider this familiar space, as well as our relationships to food and dining.

Food is, of course, a rich arena for creative investigation. It is at once so basic, so elemental, so relatable – in the sense that we all must eat to survive, and do so every day – and simultaneously so complex, rife with symbolism, an integral part of our sense of culture and identity, our rituals, our understanding of the world around us.

In this setting, Maciej Chmara and Ania Rosinke, partners both in life and work, have found inspiration for their work. In contrast to the traditional Western kitchen, they have largely interpreted the kitchen as a changeable series of objects, often more like pieces of furniture, in a variety of forms that can be customized for a number of environments, for different purposes and audiences. “Our kitchens are all a bit radical,” Chmara says, “but that’s about all they have in common. Each one has its own completely different style and rationale.”

From a beautifully handcrafted kitchen that fits on one's back (perfect for a city dweller to escape with to the countryside for an afternoon retreat) to a mobile kitchen and dining set on wheels intended to bring together strangers as an exercise in hospitality, the duo have realized concept-driven design solutions that evoke, in turn, joy, humour, grace, and even romance. Simultaneously, they have used the kitchen as a frame to pose a number of questions, big and small: What if we wholly reconsider the culture of dining? What are the real barriers between the private and public spheres? How do we facilitate and nurture community? How do we renew and feed our own souls in this context?

The Polish-born designers – who at the time of writing divide their time between Vienna and Berlin – met and began to collaborate as students at the Academy of Fine Arts in Gdańsk. They formally established their studio in Vienna in 2012, specializing in projects ranging from objects and interiors to identities and installations.

Their work is characterized by simple, poetic forms, ecological awareness and an aesthetics that frequently traces objects back to their most essential archetypes. At first glance, their pieces can seem deceptively simple; upon further inspection, though, they reveal themselves to be deeply thoughtful, intensely researched, well executed designs. While their look may be pared back, their approach is sweeping. The designers strongly believe in the modernist idea that a single individual can contribute to a variety of arenas. In other words, architects can paint and painters can create architecture; designers can illustrate, write, cook, and so on.

In 2010, were invited to create a project for the 2011 Potenziale Feldkirch. The pair wished to create a happening to encourage interaction within the community, and they decided (rightfully so) that offering free food in an unexpected setting was a great way to bring people together.

At the same time, they wanted to use the opportunity to ask a few important questions, such as: How do we treat one another – and especially strangers – in a city? How do we define the public versus the private spaces in urban settings? And how do we, individually and collectively, carve out ownership of the public space? Rosinke notes "The city space belongs to us all; we all pay for it with taxes. But we don't usually get to create or do anything unique within it."

And so *Mobile Hospitality*, the studio's first kitchen project, was born. Composed of wooden, stackable, light, and easily transportable structures – including cooking surfaces and storage, tables, folding stools, and more – *Mobile Hospitality* embraces approachable, DIY aesthetics and utility while exploring socio-cultural concerns. Chmara explains, "The people of Poland are very proud of their philosophy of hospitality. Everyone raised in Poland inherits these strict traditions of hospitality. What happens, though, when you travel to a place where you know no-one? We wanted to demonstrate our philosophy of hospitality and to provoke others into participating in urban life." To that end, they drove from place to place to set up their kitchen and spontaneously cook for – and be joined by – strangers passing by. "At our table, design meets delight and generates extraordinary opportunities to get to know each other."

They were a striking vision to be sure, wheeling their service from location to location – simultaneously familiar and surprising. As Chmara observes, it is "remarkable how the kitchen and the table together create a clear composition that transforms and defines a place completely – regardless of the setting."

Following a warm reception in Feldkirch, the pair were invited to present *Mobile Hospitality* in a number of cities over the next few years. Whether parked by a waterfront or directly in front of a city hall, they consistently drew curious diners, both the well-heeled and the down-and-out. The duo found the varying responses in different cities particularly interesting. Sometimes, their guests were quite rushed, as in New York; at other times, they were willing to linger for hours, as in Paris. Almost everywhere, there was a sense of humour in people's responses. Some diners would leave a little money because they didn't completely understand what the designers were doing. Others might run home and return with more wine to share. Without exception, though, the simple act (or perhaps the ritual) of coming together to share a meal and a moment facilitated personal connections – both among those seated at the simple wooden tables and between the guests and their hosts.

*Mobile Hospitality* opened many doors for the studio. The project attracted international attention and a number of awards. It was selected for inclusion in the permanent collections of the Museum of Applied Arts (MAK) in Vienna, where the designers also obtained a prestigious residency, and the Kunstgewerbemuseum (KGM) in Berlin. And – just as importantly – it also set the stage for the studio's subsequent kitchens, all of which, like building blocks, drew on the experiences and knowledge gained from the projects before them.

The pair's second culinary-focused work, the *DIY Vertical Kitchen* (2013), was the result of yearlong residency at the MAK. While there, they studied the history and efficacy of do-it-yourself furniture and, more broadly, DIY design culture. Inspired by the current trend of DIY furniture and furnishings, they traced the origins and evolution of the movement, testing out instructions for several noted DIY furniture projects to evaluate their accessibility and usability (or lack thereof). Their aim was to understand how realistic and/or successful benchmark DIY design projects were, and why?

The designers were surprised to learn that a number of these projects, while marketed for the masses, required a certain skill level and sometimes even special tools. Their research culminated in an exhibition and DIY furniture workshop, as well as three of their own contemporary reinterpretations of seminal DIY designs. *DIY Vertical Kitchen* revisited the 1941 *Service Wagon* by Ferdinand Kramer, reorganizing the functions vertically to improve the mini kitchen's usability. They also added new functions (a pizza oven for kicks) and made it small enough to easily fit into tiny hotel elevators. "This design was similar to *Mobile Hospitality* in many ways, but more extreme," Rosinke says. "It provided more bells and whistles, more tools, in less space; it was quite fun, and funny, really."

Soon after, in 2014, they were commissioned by Caritas, a charity in Vienna, in cooperation with the Jamie Oliver Foundation to design a kitchen for a community centre frequented by immigrant and refugee children, teenagers, and the elderly. The aim was to create a place to bring people together while educating guests about cooking and the importance of food. At the same time, the studio wished to revisit the question: How can design help foster community? The Caritas kitchen needed to be flexible to accommodate different class sizes, skillsets, and more. To that end, while the building itself was quite contemporary – all concrete and clean lines – chmara.rosinke chose to give their space a decidedly cozy, unintimidating, 1950s vibe. From the colour palette and patterned tiles to the corresponding cooking utensils (such as enamel pots with their retro feel contrasting with state-of-the-art induction plates), they chose elements intended to help make older guests in particular feel comfortable. At the same time, they designed modular, rolling workspaces that can be tucked away when unused or combined to create larger work areas. This adaptable approach extended to everything from a wheelchair-accessible workspace to the flexible electrical cables that hung from the ceiling, so guests could wheel their workspaces into a variety of configurations depending on the needs of the day. Motivated by the many needs of its diverse users, the Caritas kitchen turned an otherwise static space into a malleable, useable hub to serve and nurture a diverse community.

In parallel with the Caritas project, the studio created its fourth – and up until then most radical – kitchen for a competition organized by the Fondation Hermès. Titled *Time for Oneself*, the contest brief asked designers to rethink how people approach the concept of relaxation, and how the idea of recreation might change in the future. "This was extremely inspiring to us," Chmara recalls. "When thinking about moments of total relaxation, I remembered going fishing with my father as a small child, and what a special time that was. We would spend hours that way, doing nothing. I really like sitting by a lake; I find it meditative. It's such a big contrast to our rushed everyday lives." The sense of romantic nostalgia was palpable in the resulting design, which was conceived as "a kit to let you get away". Combining timeless craftsmanship and urban nomadism, *Time for Oneself* consists of a rucksack that transforms into a stool; inside, it holds a fishing set, grill, cutlery, and more – all handcrafted in fine materials by expert Austrian craftspeople. "This design was very emotional in a way – an exercise in transforming memories into beautiful objects. It's a celebration of crafts in a way; the formal language was all about the power of simple, beautifully executed forms. And it was quite emotional; the design of the knife, for example, was inspired by a knife my grandfather gave me when I was a child. In this way, every detail was carefully considered and meaningful."

In 2015, for the Vienna Design Week, the pair created *Cucina Futurista 2.0*, an experimental pop-up kitchen and restaurant inside the MAK. They drew direct inspiration from the 1930 culinary manifesto and radical kitchens of Italian futurist designer

Filippo Tommaso Marinetti, who saw food as an integral part of a modernist revolution and presented a radical vision spanning everything from diets to the larger dining experience. He approached dining as a total work of art – or Gesamtkunstwerk – wherein everything from the fork in your hand to the chair you sit on to the music you hear has been carefully orchestrated to create a cohesive environment. Marinetti even went so far as to have dinners wear costumes covered in unexpected, textured materials – sandpaper, cork, et cetera – and eat without cutlery to create a unique, multi-sensory stimulating experience.

In this tradition, *Cucina Futurista 2.0* asked: What might radical design for haute cuisine look like today? chmara.rosinke created everything from the tables and lighting to the tableware and the kitchen, and invited three respected chefs to collaborate on the meals. "Designers are often at their best when they have a problem to solve," Chmara points out. "By overcoming obstacles, we create more interesting results. We thought, why not do the same with chefs?" chmara.rosinke gave their collaborators strict, Marinetti-inspired briefs regarding the menu (e.g., start with a vitamin-driven course first and build up to the more pleasurable foods), and designed the kitchen equipment and the dishes with certain intentional limitations (the latter, for example, consisted of highly geometric forms, forcing the chefs to rethink food presentation entirely – and the lucky dinner guests to question the "proper" way to eat). These extraordinary parameters playfully captured the spirit of Marinetti's manifesto, encouraging the chefs to step outside their comfort zones and try something totally different.

Finally, in 2018, chmara.rosinke decided to design an updated version of their original mobile kitchen: the *Neo Modernist Kitchen*. The new design is intended to present the mobile kitchen as its own established type of furniture piece. chmara.rosinke designed it as a set of two or three modules that could easily work by themselves or together as freestanding pieces, for instance in an airy loft interior. They incorporated standard RAL colours generally applied for industrial projects (picture safety cone orange, signal yellow, traffic sign blue, and the like). By combining these industrial, essentially everyday hues in a high-end design object, the designers elevate them; they are using colours we are used to seeing in one setting and place them in a different one to tell a fresh story.

In a way, the *Neo Modernist Kitchen* also answers the question: Who are we as designers today? The new kitchen is a decidedly elegant take on the original. The duo traded in the original mobile kitchen's wooden boards for sleek painted surfaces and powder-coated aluminium; and the DIY style for a more refined visual language that better reflects their sensibility as a studio today. "The new kitchens reveal an aesthetic we've been gravitating towards in other works over the years – evident in the geometric forms, the colour palette, etc.", Chmara says. "A kitchen is something very personal in a way; it's nice to think of it as an object that can reflect your personality. Plus, we like the idea that you could easily take this piece with you when you move to a new home."

Rosinke agrees, adding, "the first mobile kitchens established the base and direction for our studio in a very clear manner; it's fun for us to see how they've evolved." And, she says, "we find it very interesting that when the word kitchen is mentioned, many people in the Western world have the same fixed image of how it looks. Most of us envision a 1940s-inspired kitchen design. We still really enjoy questioning this tendency."

In the final analysis, the kitchen series has provided the studio with a way to challenge and define themselves as designers. Looking back at the past decade's worth of projects, Chmara says: "We've learned so much along the way. But I rather feel as though we were just at the beginning, as though these past years had been a phase in our education. And there is still more education needed. That's why we continue to ask questions." He goes on "It's important to do projects once in a while in which the most important element is the act of questioning. The world is changing, but, as an industry, many of us are still basically producing the same things in repetition. It's good to try and shake things up." Rosinke agrees. "Whether the context is high end or humanitarian – Hermès or Caritas – we are presenting extreme solutions that consider different ways of approaching an everyday space. At the end of the day, we are asking questions about the ways we live."

Now what could be more delicious than that?

# Contents

This book was published on the occasion of the exhibition *mobile kitchens by chmara.rosinke* curated by Claudia Banz at the Kunstgewerbemuseum Berlin. We would like to thank the authors and everyone involved in the production of this publication.

# Essays on Kitchens

Edited by: Ania Rosinke, Maciej Chmara
Texts by: Klara Czerniewska-Andryszczyk, Warszawa
Olga Drenda, Katowice
Sarah Dorkenwald, München
Claudia Banz, Berlin
Jörg Wiesel, Basel
Agata Szydłowska, Warszawa
Anna Carnick, Berlin

Consulting: Benjamin Kaufmann
Translation p. 30-35, p. 42-46: Brita Pohl
Copyediting: Brita Pohl

Graphic design: Ania Rosinke, Maciej Chmara and Michał Pecko
Photography: Ania Rosinke and Maciej Chmara, except:
p. 14, second picture from the top: Carly Otness,
p. 16-17: Helga Traxler,
p. 28-29: Kuba Dąbrowski
p. 52-55: Courtesy of Fondation d'entreprise Hermès
Color proofing: Krzysztof Krzysztofiak
Fonts: Lato, Suisse Int'l, Objektiv MK1, TG Aqsa Pro
Printed by: Grafix, Gdańsk

Published by:
Spector Books
Harkortstraße 10
04107 Leipzig
www.spectorbooks.com

Distribution:
Germany, Austria: GVA, Gemeinsame Verlagsauslieferung Göttingen GmbH&Co. KG, www.gva-verlage.de
Switzerland: AVA Verlagsauslieferung AG, www.ava.ch
France, Belgium: Interart Paris, www.interart.fr
UK: Central Books Ltd, www.centralbooks.com
USA, Canada, Central and South America, Africa, Asia: ARTBOOK/ D.A.P., www.artbook.com
South Korea: The Book Society, www.thebooksociety.org
Australia, New Zealand: Perimeter Distribution, www.perimeterdistribution.com

© 2019 Spector Books, Leipzig
First edition: 2019
ISBN 978-3-95-905328-0

9 783959 053280